Queen Bee

7 Reasons Why Women Are Not Empowered

And What You Can Do Now To Change This Phenomenon

Bonnie McDaniel

BALBOA.
PRESS
A DIVISION OF HAY HOUSE

Copyright © 2013 Bonnie McDaniel

All rights reserved. No part of this book may be used or reproduced by any means, graphic, electronic, or mechanical, including photocopying, recording, taping or by any information storage retrieval system without the written permission of the publisher except in the case of brief quotations embodied in critical articles and reviews.

Balboa Press books may be ordered through booksellers or by contacting:

Balboa Press
A Division of Hay House
1663 Liberty Drive
Bloomington, IN 47403
www.balboapress.com
1-(877) 407-4847

Because of the dynamic nature of the Internet, any web addresses or links contained in this book may have changed since publication and may no longer be valid. The views expressed in this work are solely those of the author and do not necessarily reflect the views of the publisher, and the publisher hereby disclaims any responsibility for them.

The author of this book does not dispense medical advice or prescribe the use of any technique as a form of treatment for physical, emotional, or medical problems without the advice of a physician, either directly or indirectly. The intent of the author is only to offer information of a general nature to help you in your quest for emotional and spiritual well-being. In the event you use any of the information in this book for yourself, which is your constitutional right, the author and the publisher assume no responsibility for your actions.

Any people depicted in stock imagery provided by Thinkstock are models, and such images are being used for illustrative purposes only. Certain stock imagery © Thinkstock.

Printed in the United States of America.

ISBN: 978-1-4525-7865-1 (sc)
ISBN: 978-1-4525-7966-5 (hc)
ISBN: 978-1-4525-7866-8 (e)

Library of Congress Control Number: 2013913349

Cover design by Ariela Steif

Balboa Press rev. date: 8/30/2013

Contents

Dedication

To "Mac" - my husband, lover and best friend and the one who always made me feel empowered!

Introduction

The Phenomenon of the Queen Bee

When a young virgin queen emerges from a queen cell, she will generally seek out virgin queen rivals and attempt to kill them. Virgin queens will quickly find and kill any other emerged virgin queen, as well as any un-emerged queens. Queen cells that are opened on the side indicate that a virgin queen was likely killed by a rival virgin queen. When a new queen is available, the workers will kill the reigning queen by "balling" her, colloquially known as "cuddle death": clustering tightly around her until she dies from overheating. When a colony remains in swarm mode after the prime swarm has left, the workers may prevent virgins from fighting and one or several virgins may go with after-swarms. Other virgins may stay behind with the remnant of the hive. As many as 21 virgin queens have been counted in a single large swarm. When the after-swarm settles into a new home, the virgins will then resume normal behavior and fight to the death until only one remains. If the prime swarm has a virgin queen and the old queen, the old queen will usually be allowed to live. The old queen continues laying and within a couple of weeks she will die a natural death and the former virgin, now mated, will take her place. – Resource Wikipedia

Everybody knows one and if not, you are for certain destined to meet one. You know who she is: that female, commonly referred to as Queen Bee. Ask any woman and she will most likely have a story to share with you of an encounter with someone who fits her description.

When I began to think about the title for this book, there were many possibilities that came to mind. I needed to find a title that would not only capture the essence of what I perceive to be the problem with women's empowerment, but also suggest meaningful ways in which women can begin to build a solid foundation in order to achieve this seemingly elusive goal. What continued to come to mind and seemed to resonate with me most concerning this issue was the scientific phenomenon behind that of the queen bee.

First let me start by stating, I am not a psychologist, nor am I a scientist! Therefore, I do not pretend to know the scientific or psychological reasons behind why women are wired the way in which we are, or why we do the things we do to undermine and derail our relationships with other women. I am a woman, however, and because I wish to see this change, I will say out loud, what most of us are unwilling to admit, and that is, the real problem with women's empowerment is women! And the good news is: we also possess the power within each of us to fix it! For many years I have observed women of every age and cultural background, at work and at play and it has always been curious to me this question of how do we develop, what can be best described as, the "Queen Bee Syndrome"? Is this behavior biological or is it learned behavior?

I have broached the subject of this phenomenon with women of all colors, ages, cultural backgrounds and professions and this one thing is the common thread that appears to be consistent throughout all of womankind. As women, our biggest challenge seems to be our difficulty in effectively relating to and embracing other women. What is interesting too is that although we are very open in sharing our views on this topic one on one and in private, when in the company of a group of many women, we are more inclined to mask over what is indeed the single most pressing issue related to this topic and why we find ourselves in the position that we are in today.

Women are the masters of kissing in the air, *making pretty* when ugliness is lurking underneath the surface while not admitting to or being willing to say out loud that many of us are uncomfortable around women who are prettier, smarter, richer, thinner, in positions of power or in positions that threaten to unseat those of us who are. The truth is - we are almost guaranteed that with each encounter of another woman, we will be in the presence of someone who embodies one or more of these disarming qualities.

And because we are uncomfortable, we are also likely to assume a position of desiring to remove or destroy that thing, or in this case, that woman who is causing us to be ill at ease.

When we pretend that this problem does not exist, we continue to perpetuate the kind of behavior that has been the status quo of how we relate to each other for far too long.

In order for us to begin to realize the power of what we each bring to the universe, it is important that we change how we see ourselves and people, in particular, other women.

I get excited when I see the creative ways in which women are working to bring the message of empowerment to women, not just here in the United States, but globally. I love the prominence of the voices of women leaders who are working fervently to elevate the status of women in the fields of education, career, politics and the like.

It is my contention however, that no amount of education, seminars or empowerment workshops will ever have the level of impact needed by women in order to reach that place of empowerment, if we do not first accept that we are *broken vessels walking* and commit to changing how we view and interact with other women.

A good case in point is the recent release of Sheryl Sandberg's book *Lean In* and the rush to judgment and the willingness by several women to volunteer negative commentary before many of them had even taken the time to read and understand her message. Women, many of them in prominent positions of leadership, emerged from everywhere and like bees, swarmed in for the kill. What was particularly revealing and troubling about many of their comments was the fact that most were focused on what they perceived to be Ms. Sandberg's privileged lifestyle and background, color, education, professional position and a host of other un- important things; rather than focusing on the context of what the book is trying to say. The actions of many of these women did on many levels typify this whole idea of The Queen Bee Syndrome. What was encouraging however, was the outpouring of other women leaders who rallied in support of her powerful message. These women epitomize the kind of behavior women must seek to exhibit on every level of society when given the opportunity to step out in support of other women.

Unfortunately, it is not uncommon for those women who step up to lead, to be greeted by this kind of reaction and the big question that must be answered is WHY! There have been numerous other examples of this kind of behavior exhibited by women over time and unfortunately you only need to look as far as the latest trending headlines about any woman who has managed to pull ahead of the pack.

Queen Bee is an honest discussion about women and who we are and what is it about our species that makes us so prone to this type of behavior. Whether you are sixteen or sixty, you will be able to identify with some element of this human condition. This book is not meant to placate, but it is intended to be raw, revealing and plain in its approach. It is not meant to make the reader comfortable by *making pretty* those things that are rotten at the core, but rather to say out loud the things that are the truth about most of our opinions about other women.

It is not meant to harm, but rather to empower women in ways that will move us beyond the dream of empowerment and into a position of living and working empowered. In essence, Queen Bee is an attempt to bring about healing among women in order to allow each of us the privilege of being able to forgive ourselves and the women whom we affectionately refer to at times as our sisters.

Queen Bee will examine those issues embodied in 7 disempowering habits that women typically practice, and provide a framework through which we can begin to adopt good practices in order to help women develop skills and grow so that we can finally occupy our true places of power in the world.

Queen Bee is a book that was written to share with women how to master the art of living and working in harmony with other women, while at the same time getting what each woman wants and deserves out of life. It is a turn away from modern pervasive adversarial attitudes among women to one of women working together in a spirit of cooperativeness and supportiveness in order to finally achieve that higher and empowered goal.

Queen Bee is a gift for our mothers, daughters, sisters and friends with a message of hope for what is already ours. Open your hearts, hands and minds to receive it!

Chapter One

Self-Loathing

Turning on the Power of Falling
In Love with Who You Are

"You cannot build joy on a feeling of self-loathing!"
– Ram Dass

Turning it Off!

You cannot love what you are not! And the sad truth is most women do not love who they are!

If you have an opinion of yourself that says you are the opposite of smart, beautiful, accomplished, deserving of recognition or any of the many other attributes that most of us desire, then it is likely that you will find it difficult to admire these qualities in other women.

To make the case for this statement, let's make it personal. How many times have you looked at yourself in the mirror while naked and made the comment or had the thought of something to the effect of, I hate my thighs or my butt, or wished that you were taller, shorter or looked like someone that fits your description of beauty? And in making that comment, who was the woman that came to mind? Or how many times have you wished you were as smart as or as accomplished as another woman you know? And when you had this thought, did the mental image of this woman cause you to feel unhappy with who you are?

If you have found yourself thinking these thoughts on a number of topics and responding with statements about yourself that put you in a negative light, then, the following statement will most likely resonate with you.

When you make it a practice of focusing on and talking about what you do not have or are not, you are practicing what is known as self-loathing. And it is through this type of behavior that we begin to develop habits that lead to destructive opinions of and negative responses when interacting with other women. Over time these feelings of self-loathing become daggers that will eventually be directed at women who embody those things that we dislike about ourselves.

Here is a statement of fact. If you want to get a true sense of what a woman thinks about who she is as a person, observe how she reacts to or treats other women.

Women who do not feel good about themselves are typically catty, overly-critical of other women, find it easy to engage in negative behavior in relationship to other women and will usually not rush to be helpful if it means helping other women.

On the other hand, women who are confident in and of themselves, are at home in the company of and not threatened by other women. These types of women find it easy to compliment another woman or will not hesitate to share something that she thinks might benefit her. And by the same token, women who love the physical package that embodies that part of who they are will not feel uncomfortable when a beautiful woman enters the room. They are usually not prone to comparing themselves negatively to other women. They understand the value of measuring their own worth based upon who they know themselves to be, rather than focusing on the perceived greater value of someone else.

Years ago my sister and I took our daughters on a retreat. Joining us on the trip was one of our other nieces. One morning as we prepared to head down to the beach this niece stopped to look at herself in the mirror and began to say out loud as she moved in the style of Marilyn Monroe, "I love myself"! As she swayed from side to side, she moved her hands in a sweeping motion, across her entire body as if to affirm the person who was staring back at her in the mirror.

What occurred to me about this experience was, at the time, she was taller and perhaps a bit heavier than a lot of her peers and I am sure feeling somewhat awkward. But, for whatever the reason, she determined, at a very young age, that since this was who she was at that moment, it was incumbent upon her to fall in love with what already existed.

Ronshea was thirteen years old when this occurred, and has since grown into an independent and confident young woman. Today, she is not only very pretty to look at, but there is something remarkable about how she approaches life and her relationships with other people. Her focus is not her physical being, but rather on occupying the space that has been granted to her as her own. What was at the time perhaps just a mechanism meant to be used as a tool to disarm any negative input from other people, did in fact become the very thing that propelled her to becoming who she is today.

Bonnie McDaniel

Falling in love with who you are takes practice before you can become comfortable and accepting of oneself and it is the first step to becoming accepting of other people.

Many women have experienced all kinds of situations that have left them hurt, scarred and afraid to love what is in many of their eyes someone who is undeserving of love. The fact that so many of these women are still able to live and function day to day is a testament to the fortitude of what is innately a part of all women. Despite the past traumas, women around the world continue to rise each day filled with hope for a better tomorrow.

This tiny bit of hope, though important, is not nearly enough, however, to bring women to the place of finally owning who they are as teachers and leaders who have the capacity to change the world. In order to get there, they must first own that their existence is a special gift to the world.

Putting the Switch in the On Position

1. **Expose the naked truth about who you see as you**. Remove all of your clothes, make-up, false eyelashes, wigs, weaves, and everything that is not a part of what is naturally yours. Of course, for those women who have had permanent enhancements, they will have to leave those things in place.

   Stand in front of a full-length mirror and look at yourself as though you are being introduced to yourself for the very first time. Look deep into your eyes. Take a good look at your hair, nose, mouth, ears, lips, teeth, neck and allow yourself to continue the visual tour until you have taken in every inch of your physical design. On a blank sheet of paper, make a list of everything you like about what you see. This list should include every fine detail. In other words, do not leave anything out. Remember, you must see it to believe it!

   On another sheet of paper, list all of the things that you wish were different.

   Compare the, *I love* with the, *I wish* were different. Ask someone close to you, to make a list of all of the physical attributes that they like about you. Make a comparison of what you observed and how it differs from what you were able to see about yourself.

   Do not underestimate the power of this exercise. The truth is, you cannot change what you do not see. And you cannot see what you are unwilling to acknowledge. What you are able to recognize about those things that exist beyond the surface, that is to say your thoughts about yourself, is the truth about who you are.

When we gloss over or mask what we truly feel about ourselves, we continue to dwell in spaces that are not only, not beneficial to ourselves, but they are hazardous to the people around us. Truth is essential and liberating and it is also the first step to truly becoming empowered.

2. **Begin each day with one positive affirmation concerning the significance of who you are**. Words are perhaps the single most powerful tool that is afforded in equal proportions to everyone on the planet. A word is a word whether expressed or conceived; especially those words spoken to oneself, and the power of your words can change how you live. If you say to yourself each day that you are powerful, smart, accomplished and capable of achieving, chances are very good you will become all of these things and even more.

There is an old adage that says, "what ever comes up will come out". In other words, we tend to speak what is in our hearts. And in order to have an honest dialogue with ourselves, we must be willing to look honestly at ourselves and allow our hearts to reveal to us our truth.

Depending on where you are mentally, you may need to enlist the help of books or recordings to assist you with developing this way of thinking. I am aware of a few women who use positive music as an affirming resource by turning it on and listening before they start their day. Whatever works to get you there, use it!

3. **Surround yourself with positive people.** You will become what you consume. If you consume the energy of negative people, don't be surprised when you wake up one day and you are one of them. Negative people feed on negativity. Conversely, positive people feed on and thrive on the energy of other positive people. Spread positive energy to people around you. When you speak, smile from the inside out and watch how it changes your perspective and your interaction with others.

   As a way of identifying who fits the description of someone who is positive, spend time observing that person's approach and reactions in different situations. One piece of advice that I shared with my children was: the most effective way to gauge the true nature of a person is to pay attention to how they respond in bad situations. Do they measure their responses before reacting or are they more inclined to fly off the handle or feed into negative behavior? Are they willing to take the high road, even if they are right, rather than fighting to win at any cost just to prove they are right? There is nothing more empowering than feeding on the energy of someone who is capable of exhibiting self-control.

4. **Rather than complaining about those five extra pounds, or other things that weigh you down, make a commitment to do something about it.** Change your eating habits and put your feet into action by walking, running or dancing your way into who you want to become. Dwelling on and complaining

about something that you can easily change is a total waste of good energy and valuable time.

When you take control of your own life, you will find that the tendency to criticize and dwell on what you envy in others, will become less and less a part of how you function.

Focus your attention on the positive attributes about yourself. Learn to accentuate what you love and celebrate what you don't for the mere fact that you are alive.

I had the pleasure of interviewing a young woman a couple of years ago who had the misfortune of losing the lower parts of both her arms and legs due to contracting meningitis. This young woman went from being a star athlete to becoming a quadriplegic in a matter of days. There were moments during the fight for her life when doctors were uncertain if she would live. I asked her what it was like during that period. She shared that she experienced fear unlike anything she had ever known, but she also realized that if she could manage to get on the other side of the infection, that her life would be just fine. What was so telling about who this young woman was throughout this heart-breaking experience was not so much her ability to fight but rather her response in regards to what her next plan of action would be, knowing that she had managed to survive. When I asked her what does a person do after going through such an ordeal, her response to me was, "I DANCED"!

Today, Rayna Dubose is a powerful speaker and has the most amazing collection of shoes and prosthetics on the planet. She treats herself to regular manicures and pedicures as a way of celebrating and doing what women typically like to do, and also as a reminder to herself that each day is a blessing because she is here!

5. **Focus on what you have rather than what is missing.** A person who spends her time wishing for and looking to the future for happiness, will most likely miss the future when it arrives. Love the person that is you right now and save the one you are working toward becoming for your future celebration.

There is nothing sadder than a woman who puts her happiness and well-being on hold while she lies in wait for a future goal.

My late mother in-law was one of the most beautiful and talented women I have ever known. When I was first introduced to her at her home, at some point she sat down at her piano and began to play and sing. My husband had shared that she had made her debut at New York City's Carnegie Hall when she was just sixteen years old, but nothing could have prepared me for what I heard when she opened her mouth that day. Delores McDaniel had one of the most powerful soprano voices I had ever experienced and all these years later, I still have heard only a few voices that come anywhere near the talent that this woman embodied.

Despite her amazing talent, the world at large would never experience the beauty of that voice mainly due to her fear and her challenge with believing that she could be and have anything she could ever desire in life. She died just shy of her 60th birthday of breast cancer taking with her the gift of that beautiful voice and all the dreams she had of becoming a happy and fulfilled woman. She never knew the secret to the power of NOW!

Women have a tendency to promise themselves happiness when they achieve that state of being skinnier, richer, with a partner or without a partner, when they live or work in a certain place; and the list goes on and on. My question to these women is: WHAT ABOUT LIVING RIGHT NOW?

The power of right now is you do not have to wait! Think about it, you can choose to be happy right now. How empowering is that? You can be beautiful today in whatever jean or dress size you are right now; even if it means having to fit into a larger size. You can be happy today with another person in your life or you can be deliriously happy alone.

Several years ago a friend of mine was diagnosed with cancer. I will admit that the news of her health crisis absolutely devastated me. I garnered the courage to pay her a visit weeks after she began chemotherapy treatments. My biggest fear and what caused me to wait so long was I was not sure how to handle the change in her appearance and the reality of what it all could possibly mean. I had seen what cancer does to rob its victims of their lives and it was hard to imagine what it might do to hers.

I will never forget when she opened the door that day and the beautiful woman who greeted me, adorned in the glamorous wig covering her newly-bald head. She ushered me into the living room and began to model for me her new collection of wigs, one after the other, all while joking about how exciting it was to be able to present her husband each day he arrived home from work with a different woman.

I will forever cherish the lesson I learned from Fran Robinson that day about the importance of taking control of your life's situation and finding the joy in the moment that you are allowed to exist.

The reality of whether or not you are happy with who you are lies completely in the power of your own decision! Whether you are or are not okay with your situation is an accurate assessment; no matter which answer you choose.

6. **Forgive yourself**. Guilt is not only destructive, but it can and will paralyze you. If you have not been as kind to yourself as you feel you should have been in the past, apologize to yourself right now, learn the lesson and then, move on. Remember what is done is done and what it past is over! Do not miss the blessing of the moment that you are in now by dwelling on moments that cannot be relived. If you have made mistakes, own your mess, but don't hold on to it. Learn the lesson and let it go! Live today for the wonderful moments that are right before your eyes.

Experiencing the power of joy is elusive for a woman whose life is ensconced in guilt. Normally she will find it difficult to acknowledge the good in her life, for the simple fact that she does not think she deserves it.

Guilt has a tendency to take everything and give nothing in return. It will rob you of your todays and demand that you mortgage your tomorrows. Peace cannot dwell in a mind that is riddled with guilt and the only remedy and sure way to rid yourself of guilt is through forgiveness.

7. **Feed your mind each day**. If there is something in which you wish to become proficient, take the time to learn what you do not know. Surround yourself with knowledgeable and accomplished women. Not only will you be in excellent company, but you can also learn from their knowledge and experience. To nourish your mind, shut yourself away from the noise, and by that I mean social media, television or whatever distractions there are that prevent you from becoming completely engaged.

Take time each day to give to yourself those things that you lack intellectually. Be patient with yourself as you grow and recognize the fact that no matter what level you think you are on, when it comes to learning, each individual starts off at the same place.

What you will quickly discover is how beautiful an informed mind can make you feel. Many women experience insecurity and feel as though they don't belong and as a result they feel inadequate when in the presence of other women. Very much like having the power to change your physical appearance by exercising your body or choosing a different way of eating, you can also elevate your mental status by engaging and exercising your mind. By becoming knowledgeable, you will be able to gain a level of comfort that allows you to move about freely among other knowledgeable women. Not only will you be able to comfortably engage in interesting and stimulating conversations, but you will also be able to gain immense pleasure in listening to them as they share their knowledge and life experiences.

Keep in mind that no one is an expert in everything and the most interesting people have usually mastered just one or two things. Therefore, become a good listener and focus on the person who is sharing. What you will discover is people are very willing to share with those who are eager to listen to what they have to say. Take advantage of these opportunities to increase your knowledge in those areas that you know nothing or very little about.

Bonnie McDaniel

Exercise

1. Summarize in a short paragraph how important loving yourself is to your empowerment and to the empowerment of other women.

   _____

   _____

   _____

   _____

   _____

2. What are some of the things you need to do in order to love yourself differently and in a more nurturing way?

   _____

   _____

   _____

   _____

   _____

3. Identify the women in your life who are your positive support system and list the key elements they lend to who you are.

   _____

   _____

   _____

   _____

   _____

4. Make a list of all of the things that make you unique as a person.

_____

_____

_____

_____

_____

5. Make a list of at least three positive affirmations that you will use to empower yourself each day.

_____

_____

_____

_____

_____

6. Identify at least one new thing you will teach yourself or learn over the new 6 months.

_____

_____

_____

_____

_____

7. What thing or things will you forgive yourself for and how will you go about doing it?

_____

_____

_____

_____

_____

Chapter Two

Measuring Your Self Worth Through the Perceived Value of Other Women

Ending the Comparison Game

"Everybody is unique. Compare not yourself with anybody else lest you spoil God's curriculum"!
– Rabbi Israel ben Elizer

What Are You Worth?

You are an original!

There is no other woman on the planet quite like you. No other woman possesses your unique DNA, fingerprint, smile, mind or any of the qualities that can be identified as exclusively yours. No other woman has the ability to think like you do or do things to match your unique style.

When you occupy yourself with trying to mimic or be like another person, your actions are virtually saying to the universe, that who you are and was created to be, is of no value!

This type of thinking is at the very core of the cause of much of the animosity that exists between women. Until we are able to accept the fact that we were each given unique space on this planet to occupy and that what we each bring to the universe is equally as important as the woman next to us, we will continue to churn the same old mess and move this quest of women's empowerment exactly, nowhere!

I had a friendship with a woman that for years operated under tremendous strain. Looking back now, it is obvious to me that I continued in the relationship for so many years mainly out of habit. I also think that I lacked the courage to put both of us out of our misery by simply moving on.

Although I saw and continue to see this woman as someone who is very accomplished and talented, there were problems that existed with the value she placed on herself that simply was not enough to hold the relationship together. The sad thing was no matter what she was able to share with others through her work, she herself, never saw what others were able to recognize and that was she is amazing!

She did not like what she saw staring back at her when she looked in the mirror and in many ways she typified many of the women who fail to embrace their own beauty and unique qualities, simply because they are focused on those qualities that belong to someone else.

I spent years in the company of this woman, having to endure the brunt of her jokes and negative comments about me in an attempt on her part to take away from a person whom she, deep down inside had a tremendous amount of admiration for. After over two decades of living through the pain of maintaining a relationship with this woman, I finally decided to move on. Although my affection and admiration for the gift that she is remains, I could not continue to dwell in a space that was not nurturing and beneficial to either of us.

Women who have managed to grasp the importance of this idea of self-value are very easy to recognize. These women exude beauty from places far beyond what the eyes can see. Their understanding of who they are is undeniable and their unique physical beauty and confidence defies description. When this particular woman enters a space, she occupies that space completely. She does not walk like, talk like or "be" like anyone other than who she is.

Good examples of women who possess these qualities are women like Maya Angelou, Meryl Streep, Hilary Clinton, Jonetta Cole and the late Jean Stapleton. When you think about these women, there is something incredibly special about who they represent, and every woman's fantasy is to be given the opportunity to spend time alone with them in your presence. Your thoughts about such women as individuals do not lead you to want to compare them to anyone other than themselves. And I would contend that the reason why we are not led to want to make such comparisons is because they live and breathe only that which is uniquely their own.

There are far too many examples of women who make it a habit of devaluing what they bring to life's situations. A prime example of this type of self-deprecating woman can be witnessed in something as harmless as a paid compliment that is immediately followed up with, "oh that was nothing". Contrast that to when men are given compliments, their immediate, and seemingly natural response, is to stick out their chests and say, thank you!

There is a big difference between having, what my grandmother used to refer to as, "a big head", and acknowledging something that is indeed a fact. For example, if you took a task from conception to completion, and you did it to the best of your ability, then it is a fact that you accomplished a goal. To deflect from this fact, in order to appear humble or because you feel as though you do not deserve it, does not change the reality of or take away from the significance of what was done. There is a very famous quote by author Marianne Williamson that I read from time to time as a reminder of this truth. The quote states:

"Our deepest fear is not that we are inadequate. Our deepest fear is that we are powerful beyond measure. It is our light, not our darkness that most frightens us. We ask ourselves, "Who am I to be brilliant, gorgeous, talented, fabulous? Actually, who are you not to be? You are a child of God. Your playing small does not serve the world. There is nothing enlightened about shrinking so that other people won't feel insecure around you. We are all meant to shine, as children do. We were born to make manifest the glory of God that is within us. It's not just in some of us - it's in everyone. And as we let our own light shine, we unconsciously give other people permission to do the same. As we are liberated from our own fear, our presence automatically liberates others."

If we are to ever change the position of who we are in the world, it is important that we own and confidently occupy the space underneath our feet. We must begin to tell ourselves and believe the fact that I am in this place, wherever it might be, because I belong here.

1. **A woman who is worth her salt, knows her own value**. Knowing your value begins with knowing who you are and what you bring to the universe. Getting to know yourself requires spending time with yourself in order to discover all of what it is that makes you unique.

Many women find this difficult to do because when you spend time alone you are brought face to face with your reality. This can be especially challenging if you lack self-esteem.

Pay attention to your reactions and conversations when dealing with other people. Are you easily offended when faced with opposition? Are you inclined to react negatively when criticized by others or do you view positive, constructive criticism as a way to grow?

When you know your value, opinions by others are easily put into proper perspective and you are able to separate fiction from what is your reality.

We cannot control the opinions of others and what they might be inclined to say. We can however, control our responses when it happens.

If you are still growing in this area, make it your business to seek out a woman who can help to mentor and encourage you as you work to get there. Be very careful not to choose someone who will enable negative your behavior. Seek out and find a person who epitomizes what you hope to become and use her as an example or a goal post as you keep your eyes focused in that direction.

2. **Stay in your own lane.** One of the primary reasons why women fall into the trap of comparisons is our obsession with wanting to be who we are not. This way of thinking prevents us from being able to live an authentic life. Do not get into the habit of confusing admiration of another person with that of wanting to

abandon you in order to become who she is. Who you are has merit and unique value. When you diminish your value, you deprive others and yourself of the gifts and talents that only you can bring. Nurture and water the meadow that belongs to you rather than spending time wishing for or trying to possess that which belongs to someone else.

3. **Avoid comparison traps introduced to you by other people**. Comparisons should never be confused with compliments. The very nature of a comparison immediately suggests that one quality is superior to that of another. In this scenario, there can be only one winner and when it comes to women, you both will most likely lose.

It is not uncommon to find women using what might appear on the surface to be a compliment when comparing one woman to another. In situations such as this, this type of conversation is in reality a cloaked dagger intended to enlist negative behavior. It is unclear why we do this to one another and if I had the answer this question, I could single-handedly save the world. The question of why is not as important as my suggestion to women of why we should not engage in this type of divisive and destructive behavior. When we allow ourselves to become ensnared in this trap, our focus is turned away from the importance of the work that we a seeking to do. Instead, we become mired in emotions and the superficial, thereby diverting our attention away from what is important in favor of helping to create dissention among our peers.

When presented with this type of woman, be quick to diffuse the situation by singing the praises of the person with whom you are being compared. Point out how exciting it is to know and experience the special qualities that she brings. In other words, turn what is intended as a negative commentary into an opportunity to celebrate that person.

4. **Avoid the trap of being a people pleaser.** There is a familiar saying that goes, "you can please some of the people some of the time, but cannot please all of the people all of the time." My advice to you is - do not try! Your success in life is not contingent on whether or not others are pleased with what you do. Another person's approval or disapproval does not negate the fact that your right to exist as an individual belongs to you.

The real problem with trying to please others is that that person is in complete control of the outcome. When the controls are in the hands of someone else, the target is usually most always in perpetual motion. People who require that others please them in order to have a relationship with them, are usually those who take pleasure in manipulating others. And it goes without saying that anyone who deliberately manipulates others is only concerned with him or herself. Unfortunately, the real truth of why this person is prone to engaging in this type of behavior has everything to do with the negative view they have of themselves.

You cannot become empowered by willfully handing over your power to someone else; especially if that person is bent on misusing what she has been given.

5. **Respect authority without becoming subordinate to your own personal value.** Respect for a person because of their position over you does not mean having to subvert or undermine your personal value. It is your duty to respect and support women who are our bosses or teachers, but do not lose sight of the fact that their position has no bearing over you as a person. Be willing to support her while at the same time reminding her of your human value. And how do you do this? By positioning and presenting yourself as a working partner whose job is to positively contribute as a valued member of her team.

And if the shoe is on the other foot and you are the boss or teacher, it is incumbent upon you to be respectful and supportive to those who are working underneath your authority. Use your position to encourage and build a team of amazing future leaders.

According to an article in the March 6, 2013 issue of the Wall Street Journal psychologist Peggy Drexler wrote: "In a survey conducted by the American Management Association in 2011 from a pool of 1,000 working women, they found that 95% of women interviewed believed they had been undermined by another woman at some point in their careers."

In another study by the University of Toronto from 2008, of 1800 U. S. employees, women who worked under female supervisors, reported more instances of physical or psychological stress than in the case of those who work under the male supervisors.

There is nothing more disheartening than to witness women in authority who abuse other women. Madeline Albright once said, 'there is a special place in hell for women who refuse to help one another'. I will expand that quote by stating that there is not a hell big enough or hot enough to hold any woman who deliberately uses and abuses other women.

6. **Value your opinions, even if they are sometimes wrong.** A wrong idea or opinion is an opportunity to learn from your mistakes. Without the benefit of a wrong opinion, you will never be able to get a gauge on your successes in life. Do not allow anyone to dismiss your ability to contribute simply because you made a mistake.

   There is not a person alive who has not at one time or another, made a wrong turn or failed to exercise good judgment, so accept the fact that you are not alone.

   Do not spend time beating up yourself when you make a mistake – acknowledge it, capture the lesson and move on. By the same token, do not allow others to dwell on your mistakes as a way of devaluing who you are. When faced with a person who wants to focus on your errors, immediately take control by acknowledging your mistake, followed up by what you learned from the experience and how you plan to move forward.

7. **Steer clear of people who deplete you.** Wells are meant to give water, but in order to give water, they

must be consistently filled. If you find yourself in the company of someone who is constantly taking from and never giving back to you, find yourself a new friend. A person to whom it never occurs that you are as deserving of receiving a gift as well as imparting one, is what many refer to today as an emotional vampire.

This type of person does not abide by the rules of reciprocity. They are usually of the opinion that the only way to progress in life is by grabbing everything they can and leaving nothing for others who will follow. They find it difficult to grasp the concept of living with open hands. My grandmother and mother taught me this concept very early in life, and that is, in order for one to receive or to give gifts, you must live with open hands. It is important to remember that when each person gives, everyone benefits.

Exercise

1. Define your value?

   _____

   _____

   _____

   _____

   _____

2. What habits must you break in order to end the cycle of negatively comparing yourself to other women?

   _____

   _____

   _____

   _____

   _____

3. Who are you? Write a description of who you perceive yourself to be.

   _____

   _____

   _____

   _____

   _____

4. Identify that person within your circle who habitually compares you in a negative way to other people. Determine how you will handle the next time it occurs.

_____

_____

_____

_____

_____

5. What response will you give in the future when you are placed in the position of being disrespected by a boss, friend or superior? Limit your answers to only what applies to this question, in other words do not make it personal.

_____

_____

_____

_____

_____

6. Identify those people around you with whom after interacting with them leave you drained. How will you alter your interactions with them in the future?

_____

_____

_____

_____

_____

7. List at least three things that you think are important to being able to recognize your worth or value.

_____

_____

_____

_____

_____

Chapter Three

Ineffective Use of Words

Practicing Good Language

"Speak clearly, if you speak at all; carve
every word before you let it fall"!
– Oliver Wendell Holmes

The Trap

You would perhaps think that for someone who founded an organization that encourages women to talk, that given the complexity of this topic, that conventional wisdom would suggest that I steer as far away from this subject as possible. And as much as I agree with the fact that more wars are created with words than weapons, it is a war that women, no matter what her age, race or cultural background, must fight in order to achieve this goal of empowerment.

Positive words between, about and toward women by women is a powerful weapon that can be used to change the plight of women around the world for generations to come. The key however, is in how we engage and choose to use them. If I am to have the impact that I believe talking can elicit on the culture of modern women, the way in which we talk to and about one another has to change.

Having said that however, I would contend that as powerful a weapon as words are to resolving this issue of women's empowerment, it is also the one thing that could ultimately derail all of the hard work and sacrifice that has been made by women over the course of many generations.

In 2008, I realized after a few years of facilitating gatherings where women could talk and have a positive impact on one another, that words could be used to help to remove the barriers that have been for so long, ensconced in our fight to becoming empowered. That realization led to the launching of an initiative called, Women Are Talking. My reason for wanting to organize women in such a fashion had everything to do with my belief that when women come together and have a good conversation, our words have the power to change the world.

As much as I subscribe to this notion, I also know that this will be as challenging an effort as I have ever undertaken in my quest to lend my part to the cause of women's empowerment. And until women from every walk of life are able to grasp the power of words, we will continue to miss the mark in realizing the dream.

We live in a society where anything spoken negatively is given center stage. Conversely, women who are working through good dialogue to effect positive change in the world are very often drowned out by negative noise. It is especially disheartening when you witness intelligent women who feel the need to resort to the use of negative references, in order to make their voices heard. And it is equally as disheartening when women who know the difference join in the negativity to drown out the good of what these women have to say.

If we are to rise above the things that are holding us back, we must be willing to create a nurturing space and support positive women in order to elevate their voices to a platform where they can be heard and bring about change in the world.

Another very common and destructive practice in which women consistently engage is gossip. I am not sure what it is about spreading negative hearsay that causes women, in particular, to latch onto and feed on this type of behavior. The interesting thing about this aspect of the Queen Bee Syndrome is that our entire way of engaging one another through modern technology is contingent on the very fact that we are drawn to sharing what we have heard with another person. Imagine, if you will, a world where the power of the tools that have been afforded to us are instead employed to focus on and empower women everywhere who are seeking to and doing good things.

Far too many women are willing to use this practice as a way of leveling the playing field when in competition with another woman. In many instances it never occurs to them that the most effective way of elevating themselves is to elevate the woman who is at the head of the line. When you elevate another person, a vacuum is created, thereby providing an opportunity for you to step into and fill that space.

Change the Tone and Direction of the Conversation

1. **Let Your Words Reflect the World You Wish to Create for All Women.** There are two types of people in the world. People who write the script and people who follow along with whatever is being said. Therefore, the first step to changing the dynamics of how women talk is to determine in which conversations you will or will not engage. The interesting thing about conversation is the unique ability we each have to steer it in a positive direction. In order to determine the direction or value of the discussion, ask yourself these three things before repeating: is it true, is it constructive or is it beneficial to the end game.

   In 2008, Sarah Palin was introduced as the Vice-Presidential nominee for the Republican Party. I remember being in my car when she delivered her first message to the country. As I listened to her speech, I remember thinking to myself, what a powerful woman. Regardless of whether or not you differed with her political viewpoints, at that moment you could not dismiss the impact she had on the political landscape. She managed, for a short while, to rally the party and she became on icon in American politics.

   Unfortunately, as in the history of what has happened to so many women who came before her, the conversation concerning her prospects within a few short months began to change. The focus quickly became one of how much was being spent on her clothing, what she ate, where she lived and other things that lend themselves to taking the conversation off topic. Perhaps the most telling thing about this experience was having the unfortunate opportunity of witnessing how a lively debate of who was qualified to lead the American people could so quickly turn into what women should or should not wear while running for political office. It is important to note that this example is not to elicit a discussion about whether or not Sarah Palin should have been allowed to make her way to the White House, but rather, the process we go through in order to choose women leaders.

2. **Avoid listening to or spreading gossip**. Gossip is perhaps the single most toxic activity in which women habitually engage. This activity has the power to ruin reputations, create wars, derail good causes and create irreparable damage that can have impact on the progress of women over many generations.

This type of behavior begins very early with girls typically around adolescence. For whatever the reason, girls begin early to try to confirm who they are by diminishing their peers. Boys also participate in this type of rivalry behavior, however, boys play for marbles while girls play for hurt feelings. It is not uncommon these days for certain girls to suffer at the hands of what is characterized as "mean girls" as they seek to establish their place in the world. Unfortunately a lot of this activity can become quite vicious and with the availability of the internet and social media, what was once confined to school and the playground has now expanded to include a much larger stage. In a matter of seconds a relatively small exchange can escalate into a viral virtual war.

During one of my Sunday school classes of 7th and 8th graders, I led a discussion on the negative impact gossip can have on a person's life. One of the girls in the class asked when was it okay to share negative information. She went on the say that she had used it as a way of getting back at someone who was trying to steal a boyfriend. Her method of getting back was troubling but typical as she spread a rumor among her friends who then spread it around the school that this particular girl was a "whore". I asked her to define the word. I went on to ask if based upon what she knew to be fact and not hearsay, if the description of whore was an accurate depiction of her classmate. She agreed that it was not. It is important that when presented with a situation such as this that a person who knows the proper response steps up and help the person to adopt different behavior.

There is a big difference between sharing facts and spreading information as a way of causing harm. To help with distinguishing between sharing and gossip, here is how the dictionary defines gossip. According to Meriam-Webster, gossip is defined as, casual or unconstrained conversation or reports about other people, typically involving details that are not confirmed as being true. Gossip is also used as a way of slandering, thereby, causing others to view that person in a negative light.

Many women will use gossip to undermine other women when they feel threatened and wish to eliminate what they perceive as a threat or competition. In interviewing several male executives, a few of them shared that in the professional arena, a sharp male will typically sit back and wait while females destroy each other and as a result, never have to lift a finger to move a rival out of the way. In other words they pit women against each other to advance their own cause. Women have to become smarter and recognize that destroying each other is not the way to empowerment.

If you find yourself drawn into a situation such as this, the most effective way to diffuse or shut it down is to pose the following question to the tale-bearer, "what can we do to help her"? In nine out of ten instances, the person who is spreading the gossip will most likely make a quick exit.

3. **When something positive happens in the world of women, be the first to share the good news**. In today's world of technology, things can happen in an instant! With so many wonderful tools afforded to us such as twitter, Facebook, Pinterest, Linkedin, blogs, and a host of other tools, we can have an impact on the advancement of women in ways never imagined just a few short decades ago.

As women, we must utilize whatever tools we have available to us as a means of pushing forward our quest for empowerment and in support of each other. Whenever you read or hear something positive that has been accomplished by other women, take the opportunity to utilize your network to share and shed a light on their accomplishments. When you share this kind of information, you become a catalyst for helping to change how women are perceived and accepted in the world. By sharing, you also encourage other women who are striving to become leaders to keep moving ahead. Remember when we are able to see the vision, we can achieve the goal.

4. **Create a space where women can be encouraged**. Every woman should have the benefit of being able to visit a space where she is accepted, supported and encouraged. This space should be absent of judgment, a place where women can share ideas, resources and experiences and this type of environment should be the norm rather than the exception.

   It has been proven that people, women in particular, are more apt to thrive where they are nurtured. It is important for those women who have been given the benefit of attaining positions of leadership, to commit to being that sounding board that is so desperately needed by up and coming professionals in order to help lay a foundation for a successful path in their careers.

5. **Make the case for women – become an active advocate.** Whenever you have the opportunity to help push the agenda of another woman, be the first to speak up! With over 50% of the world's population consisting of women, there is absolutely no reason why our voices should ever be muted. We have a responsibility to make certain that every voice of every woman from every corner of the earth is given the opportunity to fall on listening and supportive ears. We can achieve this through education, advocacy and effective leadership through women in leadership positions.

6. **Be an example to your peers of how to verbally engage other women.** When verbally engaging others, choose your words wisely. The choice of one word over

another can determine the negative or positive outcome of almost any situation. When you speak, be careful of things such as your inflection or tone and make sure not to over-emphasize or exaggerate a point; especially in those instances where your comments can be taken out of context. If you find yourself in a situation where you have been drawn into a conversation that has become inflamed, restate the comment as a way of allowing the person who made it to consider what has been said. There is also another good approach of just allowing the conversation to die a natural and deserving death. Another effective tool that works wonders is to turn on the magic of your smile.

7. **Lend her your ear.** One of the most effective things you can do to boost another woman's agenda is to listen to what she has to say. There is something amazingly powerful about allowing another woman to state her case out loud to an audience of women. It is especially empowering when those words are able to land on supportive ears.

   When given the opportunity, be that sounding board in order to encourage and support women around you. To listen effectively, make a concerted effort to completely engage yourself by putting aside any distractions that might convey disinterest or a lack of support.

   A good way to maintain focus is to take notes and ask appropriate questions as a way of helping the conversation along. When posing questions, be sure to offer positive comments as a way of stressing the importance of her message and to provide the lift that perhaps is needed.

Exercise

1. Write a description of what you would like to see happen in the world in regards to women. What actions can you take to contribute?

   _____

   _____

   _____

   _____

2. List instances in which you have engaged in malicious gossip against another woman and determine what actions you will take to change your behavior in the future?

   _____

   _____

   _____

   _____

3. Identify situations where you can help to spread the word about something good that is happening in the lives of other women. How will you use your network to engage others on their behalf?

   _____

   _____

   _____

   _____

4. What connections do you personally have that could serve as a positive space to encourage and support women around you?

_____

_____

_____

_____

_____

5. What skills do you possess that could lend themselves to creating a positive dialogue between groups of women?

_____

_____

_____

_____

_____

6. How good are your listening skills? Write an assessment of how well or how poorly you think you listen. If there is room for improvement, what course of action will you take to change it?

_____

_____

_____

_____

_____

7. Are you a good advocate for women? If not, what things can you do in order to become a more positive force?

_____

_____

_____

_____

_____

Chapter Four

Making it Personal

Focusing on What Matters

"If women are to redesign our lives,
we must reshape our focus"
– unknown

4

Personal Matters Do Not Matter

When women approach almost any subject or situation, we have a tendency to focus on things that are not important. When we meet another woman, our thoughts will typically gravitate to things like, is she pretty or thin; we analyze what she is wearing and depending on how we feel at that moment, our lack of focus may cause us to miss a real opportunity for the simple fact that we are focusing on the wrong things. In order to make the most of empowering moments, we must take our focus away from the superficial. I know this is perhaps going to inflame a lot of women, but in order to fix a problem we have to be willing to state the truth. Women are indeed smart, accomplished and capable of achieving anything we set our minds to doing. The key is to set our minds on the right things.

We were born with qualities that are unique and special to each of us and us alone. The fact that someone is different should never be the focus of whether or not she is capable or deserving of your support.

During my participation in a panel discussion with a group of young women professionals, I took the opportunity to observe them as they filed into the room. In particular, I focused my attention on their interactions with one another. As each woman entered she looked around the room as if to check out each of the other women. The expressions on their faces told a story about what she might have been thinking about each of the other women. What was interesting is the prettier the young woman, the more interesting the expressions on the faces of the other women.

Once we began I asked each of them to stand and turn to the woman on her left, smile while extending her hand, state her name and share something amazing about herself. They were then asked to turn to the person on the right and do the same. What was so interesting about this exercise is that it changed the atmosphere in the room. Once they spoke to each other, what was at the beginning of the session a room filled with women with preconceived and perhaps negative notions about the person suddenly turned into a welcoming exchange. Once the session was over, I also noted the excitement among the women of wanting to learn more about each other and the interest in staying connected. There were even a few instances where vital connections were made.

External dressings are simply coverings for the truth of what lies underneath in the heart of every woman. If we are to truly engage and support one another, it is incumbent upon us to cease operating with surface material.

Just the facts!

1. **Approach each new introduction and situation with a blank canvass.** When meeting a woman for the first time, resist the urge to paint a picture of who she is with ideas either prematurely formulated by you or suggested by someone else.

   Each person is a unique individual, with different ideas and experiences. Therefore, each individual deserves to be treated based upon her own merit and your experience with them. When we paint inaccurate pictures of others due to our own inadequacies, insecurities or misinformation, we interrupt the process of being able to make a good connection. Women who spread inaccurate assessments about other women are especially troubling and for those who are on the receiving end, it is important that you shut it down by refusing to listen to her opinion. If it is a criticism of the other woman, ask instead, "what can we do the help her"?

2. **Have an agenda**. Before meeting someone new, make a list of three positive things that you wish to learn about the person and focus on those things at the outset of the meeting. Where possible, learn as much as you can in advance by doing research using resources such as Google or other references where information might be available. This will help to prevent you from making hasty assessments as well as provide positive structure for the conversation. In addition to information that you have learned, be sure

to keep your mind open and actively listen to what she has to say.

3. **Partition negative feelings.** Like every other human being, women are a product of their experiences which means we bring who we are and our baggage as a result of those experiences into every situation. It can be expected that there will be times when our responses to certain people and situations will be less than admirable. This can be expected because we are human. When faced with a situation where your emotions are threatening to color your opinion, acknowledge what you are feeling, separate your emotions from what is and is not fact and work your way through. In certain instances it might be helpful to enlist a trusted co-worker or confidant to help bring your focus back to where it needs to be.

4. **Become an active supporter.** Nothing takes away fear like diving into uncertain territory head first. To do this, rather than focusing on what can you gain, look for ways in which you can give – to the other person. Far too often, women will greet a new person by immediately erecting a wall which starts the conversation off on the wrong footing. By taking a positive approach, you immediately place the power within your hands to steer the conversation in the right direction. Whoever gives most to a situation controls the outcome.

Ask specific questions about how you might be able to support her efforts. In other words, establish how you can become a "helper". To demonstrate your interest and support, be sure to take notes and if you are led, make a commitment to actively lend your support, making sure that whatever you commit to doing that you follow through.

One of my many roles as a supporter of women is to create and facilitate workshops focused on the subject of empowerment and personal development. Recently I was asked to create a workshop for a conference geared toward young women who are seeking to enter political office. The workshop was focused on helping to build a sisterhood. To teach the lesson I created a workshop using the acronym H.E.L.P.E.R. To be a helper is to be of service, provide aid or relief, to be responsible for, to assist in an action, to promote, to give without requesting anything in return.

In order to be the kind of support needed in order to empower and become empowered, women must learn how to become helpers of other women.

5. **Use empowering language.** When speaking to another woman make a concerted effort to choose words that empower. Resist the urge to criticize and steer clear of negative references. If you find it necessary to speak on something that can be viewed as negative, use the sandwich approach by beginning and ending with something positive.

   Use phrases such as: *you inspire me,* or *I am so happy we met;* or anything that lets the other person know that you are positive about the connection.

6. **Admit and accept when it does not work and move on.** Not every relationship was meant to be.

If you find yourself in the presence of someone and it just is not working, be as polite as possible, thank them for the privilege of meeting them and make your exit. Accept the fact that there will be instances where two people are not going to get along. Do not make the unfortunate experience of your encounter a topic of discussion with others, instead, allow the next person the opportunity to have their own experience. Just as no two people are alike and will have different perspectives on any given topic, meetings and interactions with others will be completely different with different people.

The one good thing about being kind is it costs absolutely nothing! Therefore kindness should always be your first line of defense. What is interesting too is it is possible that the timing is off for having a relationship at that time. By making a good exit, you leave the door open for a possible future exchange.

7. **Learn from and build on each new experience.** It is a wise person who looks for the lessons to be learned from each experience. Not only do we gain knowledge but different kinds of experiences add valuable texture to what would ordinarily be a very ho-hum existence. Some of the most interesting people I have ever met have been those whose lives reflect experiences from every possible vantage point.

    If you have find yourself in a situation where you would rather be anywhere but where you are, do not make it personal. Focus instead on what value it can bring to your life experience.

Use the time spent as a way of exploring uncharted territory. Ask questions to learn about something that is totally new to you. By expressing your interest in the other person's knowledge, not only will you learn something different, but you are also likely to gain an ally.

Exercise

1. What things do you immediately pay attention to when meeting a new person?

   _____

   _____

   _____

   _____

   _____

2. What steps do you take to begin the conversation?

   _____

   _____

   _____

   _____

   _____

3. What steps can you take to partition negative feelings toward someone whose reputation preceded you meeting them?

   _____

   _____

   _____

   _____

   _____

4. How can you use your talents to become a "helper"?

_____

_____

_____

_____

_____

5. Create a list of empowering words that you will use to empower women around you.

_____

_____

_____

_____

_____

6. What are the key things needed in order to walk away from a situation that is not good for you and leave the door open for a possible future exchange?

_____

_____

_____

_____

_____

7. What key things should you look to learn from each new experience?

_____

_____

_____

_____

_____

Chapter Five

Unwillingness to Mentor Other Women

Paying it Forward

"The greatest good you can do for another is not just to
share your riches, but to reveal to him his own"!
– Benjamin Disraelli

The Mentor Challenge

Everyone had to travel to get to where they are in life and no one gets there alone. One of the key elements to women becoming empowered is for each woman to make a commitment to take the time to share their knowledge and experiences through mentoring other women. When it comes to the power of mentoring there is no substitute. Formal education can provide you with subject matter knowledge but it is only through gleaning lessons from the experiences of others that knowledge truly comes to life.

Every woman, whether she has had the benefit of being mentored or not, has a duty and responsibility to pour back into the next generation a portion of what she has learned over the course of her career.

Unfortunately, too many women take the attitude of, I got mine, therefore, get your own, thereby missing a great opportunity to impact the cause for women on a much broader scale. When we deprive other women of our knowledge and experiences we short-circuit the path to women's empowerment.

When I entered my first position in the field of technology, I started out in an office that was primarily white and male with the exception of one woman. Before assuming that role, I had never known another woman, in particular an African American woman who worked in that field. On the first day in my new role I made my way to the female account executive's cubicle to introduce myself since, she, unlike all of her male counterparts chose to forgo my welcome. When I extended my hand to introduce myself she did the oddest thing. She gave me a blank stare as if to silently ask, "why are you here"? To make matters worse she never said a word and resumed doing what she was doing before I entered her space. I tried on a few occasions to be friendly or ask questions in an attempt to engage her in conversation, but each time she gave me the same blank stare and said nothing. One day we both happened in the ladies room at the same time and I confronted her asking the question of why was it that she did not seem to like me. Her answer of, "I don't know", said it all. In her mind she was the chosen one, this had been her space before I showed up and she was at a loss as to what to do about it. She had never had the benefit of knowing how to handle a situation such as this; one in which she felt threatened and afraid of losing ground that she had worked so hard to gain. I never had a chance to figure out if she had ever had the benefit of being mentored by another woman, but I would venture to guess that she had not. We never did get a chance to bond, as she left the company soon thereafter. Six months after I joined the organization, I had my chance to do for the woman who was later hired, what was not afforded to me.

This important lesson of sharing had come through an experience that I had had early in my professional career, long before I entered professional sales. In my first job fresh out of college, I was hired by a major corporation as the assistant director of public relations. Very much like the technology situation years later, I was only the second woman and only African-American to be hired in that position. The woman who had spent many years with the company in that department before I arrived was less than welcoming. As a result, I never received the benefit of her experience and knowledge and subsequently had to pretty much figure things out on my own. The question of whether or not she was obligated to teach me anything is not relevant. What was relevant, however, was the loss of a great opportunity for her to shine as a leader.

My boss, who also became my first professional mentor, encouraged me by suggesting that I take time to take notes and assess the situation carefully and learn what I could from it. And, he went on to add that when it came my turn to share with women who would follow in my path, that I take the opportunity to do things differently. What wonderful advice.

So many women do and say things against other women without understanding why. We react negatively because we are uncomfortable and our primitive instinct is to have anything that threatens or make us uncomfortable go away.

The Queen Bee Syndrome is one that operates under the premise of exclusivity which means there can be only one instead of recognizing that it is beneficial and empowering to the cause of women when others are provided equal access. This way of thinking is especially prevalent among African-American women. There have been numerous occasions where I have had the unpleasant experience of being greeted by visceral reactions when entering a space that had previously been occupied by the first or only African American woman. The reasons for this kind of reaction are steeped in a lot of our history and have been passed down for generations. It is in the best interest of women, the African American community in particular, that this type of behavior ends. It is especially concerning since within our communities it is hard for us to imagine more than one woman being allowed to occupy a revered space at a time. The fact that we would limit ourselves by buying into this way of thinking is in and of itself not a good strategy. After all the African-American community is filled with so many amazing women and just as in the female population at large, we cannot afford to be denied the benefit of their talent. In defense of African American women, it is understandable why this exists as it is probably true that the path to achieving individual success has not been an easy journey. When questioned as to why, many shared that they had experienced racism, sexism and had to fight every step of the way to get to where they are. Anyone who has had to endure such a journey is not likely to want to make it a ski ride for the next person coming up in the ranks. Although one can sympathize with this, we cannot afford to use this as an excuse for perpetuating a system that serves no one. When a woman earns the right to be in a place, it is not only discouraging, but also disrespectful to her to have to experience what is essentially reverse discrimination simply because of someone else's past hurts. The mold must be broken and there is no better place than to have it begin with you.

By adopting the practice of equal access, the number of women in positions of authority increase thereby creating opportunities that can positively impact women for generations to come.

It is incumbent upon today's women leaders to teach the next generation of young women how to mentor by defining mentorship in both how we think and lead.

Pay it Forward

1. **Teach what you know**. Knowledge has no real value until it is shared with someone else. This should not be confused with asking to be paid fairly for your work. To be clear, women should be compensated for the skills and knowledge they bring to the table in the professional arena. However, having said that, there should be a way in which she can share the benefit of that knowledge as a way of advancing the cause for women. In other words, when what you know has the ability to change the course of and impact the lives of others, it should not be kept to yourself. By sharing your knowledge you open up a world of possibilities to not only spread your message but also have tremendous influence on our culture.

   The more you share your knowledge with up-and-coming women leaders, the more you level the playing field for women who are coming up in the rear. The more women are allowed to lead, the easier it will become for the world to see them as viable leaders.

2. **Model by doing.** Young women are impacted most not so much by what you say, but what they see you do. Whether or not it is apparent, young or inexperienced women are watching you. They are looking for cues on how to do simple things like walk, talk, respond to others, work and even play in a professional environment. It is not uncommon to meet young women who have earned degrees and yet lack some of the more important social skills that are needed when operating around and engaging others. What is

not taught in a lot of institutions, are the soft human skills that can gain you access into the executive board room if you have them, or can cause you to be shown the door post-haste, if you do not.

I majored in Business Administration in college and one of the most valuable courses I studied was a course entitled, The Art of Gracious Living. This course was a requirement for anyone majoring in business and it has served me extremely well over the years. Because of the knowledge I gained in this class and at home, I have never been at a loss for the right response or proper conduct in any situation involving other people on any level. I have in the past, shared this information through etiquette or protocol classes and because I so strongly believe in the impact this can have on the lives of the next generation of leaders, I will continue to highlight the importance of these skills in my on-going work for women and girls. I will add too, that this knowledge has also been supplemented in ways that I cannot begin to measure, by women and men mentors that I had the benefit of engaging along the way.

For women who are equipped in these areas, make it a part of what you do to mentor and watch how it changes the confidence level of young women. When women are comfortable with who they are, they are unstoppable.

Unfortunately, because there are not nearly as many women in positions of leadership, there are not enough examples of how women should conduct themselves once they are allowed access. And because women leaders operate in what is essentially a fish bowl, it becomes even more important that their actions model the right path to leadership for the women coming up in the ranks.

3. **Move to the head of the line.** Being gracious is admirable, but not if it means slinking back when you have earned the right to be in a leadership position. It is interesting that in this day and age, women continue to struggle with assuming their rightful places in the world. It is not uncommon for women to delay the answer to the call when leadership opportunities are presented. Many of us make the unfortunate assumption that if we work hard that the reward will equal our merit and that we will somehow magically be given what we deserve. The truth is in most competitive situations, the two operate exclusive of each other. If you have earned the right to lead, make no deference when it comes to occupying the space that is already yours.

   By having the courage to step up, you set the bar in a position for other women to be able to reach and raise the standards for attaining even higher goals. Make an effort to identify women who are coming up in the ranks, who are either connected to you within your organization or through connections with women who are in similar positions. Take time to share what you have learned in reference to what she should or should not do when trying to move ahead.

   Keep in mind that your insight into any given situation may not be the end all, so listen closely for cues from the other person who might be able to lend a very different perspective. I have learned some of my most valuable lessons from these experiences. Remember, working together as a team is always the best approach.

4. **Give without expecting anything in return**. A gift is not a gift until it is given away. Mentoring is a willful act to generously share your gift of knowledge and experience in order to empower others. The expectation is that what you give will impact and influence the life of another individual. Mentoring is a commitment and should be taken seriously, therefore weigh what will be required of you before engaging to do so.

It is not only discouraging to someone who is counting on your help if you do not live up to your commitment, but it can also impede her progress. It is better to not commit than to commit and not follow through.

If you are introduced to someone who could benefit from your guidance and you are unable to commit to her at the time, seek out other colleagues or contacts who might be able to step in. Mentoring between women really does require a village and the village works best when everyone takes part. Be sure to explain to your proxy exactly what is needed and gain her commitment to dedicate the time before making the connection between the two.

Use this opportunity to explain to the mentee the importance of paying it forward and the huge impact it can have on women's empowerment. In other words, make it clear that what is given to her should be passed on to the next woman in line.

5. **Seek out opportunities within your network to help other women to advance**. The good old boys club is good because they know how to use it to their benefit. Men have mastered the art of grooming other men to assume positions of leadership as they move up in the ranks, primarily because they have been taught how. They understand the concept of seeding the field with players who will support their own leadership. A true power base is built from within the ranks by identifying and surrounding yourself with other capable women.

   It is a well-known fact that many women are reluctant to taking this approach because of the issues of distrust and the fact that we have not been at it long enough to know that it works and works well. It is important for women to recognize that as with most things, there is always a risk when bringing someone into what is essentially fertile personal space and that risk is not relegated to gender. We cannot afford not to support other women simply because we fear that they may advance to the front of the line. The benefits clearly outweigh any risk that might exist.

   Be selective and choose someone who is willing to be coached. Never force yourself on someone who is not ready or not receptive to your offer of help. Make sure to approach from a standpoint of partnership and teamwork and consistently stress her value to the overall success to the effort.

6. **Share resources outside of the office.** An experienced woman knows that most good connections are made outside of the office rather than between the

hours of nine and five. This is especially true for women entrepreneurs who face a different set of problems than her sisters who are employed by someone else.

Women entrepreneurs find it especially tough simply because unlike their corporate counterparts, they usually operate very much alone. The competitive nature of being in business for oneself makes it hard to find other women in the same kind of business who are willing to mentor you. Unlike when you are working for someone else, your livelihood depends on whether or not you are able to daily add to your bottom line. Therefore, it is difficult for most women to embrace the idea of mentoring someone who could very easily put them out of business. There are some exceptions, but these exceptions are not the norm.

In situations such as this, it helps to reach out to women who are seasoned business owners or better yet, ones who are retired to ask for guidance. These women are typically more willing and in most instances, very eager to share what they know with other women. As with their male counterparts, many of these retired women are honored to know that their knowledge still has relevance and will usually commit to spending whatever time is needed in order to get the job done.

If you are a seasoned or retired professional or entrepreneur, seek out opportunities to mentor by connecting with young women's organizations, of which there are many, in order to make them aware of your willingness to share your knowledge. These types of organizations are always looking for resources to share with their members.

7. **Invite other women mentor groups to join in.** Seek out women who are providing mentoring to other women to meet up with up-and-coming professionals after hours. This can be very effective as it helps to build much-needed bonds within the professional community. This also provides a way in which women can connect with their peers.

Fortunately, there have been a number of women leaders who have recognized the value of women mentoring other women and have founded some amazing organizations that are leading the charge on this front in a major way. A list of some of these organizations, are provided in the resource section of this book.

Exercise

1. What skills or talents do you have that you can use to teach or encourage other women?

    _____

    _____

    _____

    _____

    _____

2. What is your definition of someone who is a good role model? Make a list of women who are in the public eye who are good role models.

    _____

    _____

    _____

    _____

    _____

3. What leadership qualities do you possess that could help you to assume a leadership role? Identify an area where you could step up and lead.

    _____

    _____

    _____

    _____

    _____

4. How do you give back to women's organizations or causes and how can you increase your efforts in the area of "give-back"?

_____

_____

_____

_____

_____

5. What are you doing to build the "sister-hood" within your own personal network? Define what it means to be a h.e.l.p.e.r.

_____

_____

_____

_____

_____

6. What qualities do you possess that could help you to become a mentor?

_____

_____

_____

_____

_____

7. How can you use your social life as a way of connecting and serving other women?

_____

_____

_____

_____

_____

Chapter Six

Reluctance to Collaborate with Other Women

Teaming to Win

"We are not self-made. We are dependent
on one another. Admitting this to ourselves isn't
an embrace of mediocrity and derivativeness, it's
a liberation from our misconceptions."
– Kirby Ferguson

6

Fear of the Connection

Two heads are always better than one except when you fail to make full use of the one that is sitting right in front of you. Collaboration is one of the most effective ways available to women to make the kind of impact and progress needed in order to achieve the dream of empowerment.

When women work together, not only are they able to distribute the weight or burden that comes with trying to achieve a goal, but they are also able to benefit from the collective knowledge and resources that collaboration brings.

The very notion of collaboration suggests that there be a certain level of trust, cooperation and the sharing of resources and power between women in order to achieve a common goal. It also means relinquishing the spotlight that would ordinarily be focused on one to that of being shone on many.

Throughout the course of history, it has been the dream of women leaders to reach that individual pinnacle of success. Many of these women have sacrificed in ways unimaginable and therefore have earned the right to occupy center stage and be rewarded for a job well done.

Unfortunately, in our fast-moving, competitive world, the stakes are high and lone wolves don't achieve nearly the level of success as those who make the commitment to work in partnership with others.

When we fail to work together, our impact loses its overall effectiveness, essentially becoming a watered down version of what could have been amazing. It is important that women adopt a mindset that causes us to actively seek ways to combine forces in order to effectively advance the cause for women.

It is easy to understand the reluctance on some women's parts and their desire to steer clear of trying to work with other women. The history of women working together, on a large scale, has been proven to be somewhat of a challenge. A lot of the challenge has come about as the result of our focusing on things that have very little or nothing to do with the goal. We have a tendency to bring personal matters into the discussion which is a certain death when trying to work toward advancing a collective agenda. As women we must put aside the negative competition that raises its head far too often thereby taking our minds off of the ultimate prize.

In my interviews with women on this topic, what I found was this issue exists between women of all ages, cultural backgrounds, and ethnic groups, within and outside of family units; in other words it is deeply woven into the fabric of who we are as women.

I also spoke to several male executives who shared their experiences with women team members who openly expressed their desire not work with other women. This is particularly troubling because when we stand up and demand equality for women and yet suppress the efforts of other women, it sends a message of dysfunction and confusion among women and subsequently pushes the cause for women in the wrong direction.

The issue of collaboration is one that is critical if we are to get beyond where we are currently in the quest for empowerment. It is an issue that needs to be discussed openly with the commitment to not only talk, but actively seek to bring about a positive resolution. It is not pretty, but as with most problems, the key to getting beyond the problem is to admit that it exists.

Several months ago I had the opportunity to attend one of the many events held during Women's History Month. This event highlighted many of the female icons who over the course our history helped to frame and advance the cause for women. It was an evening that was filled with celebration and provided the opportunity to listen to some of the top women leaders in the country issue a call to action for what needs to happen next.

At the conclusion of the ceremony, I spent extra time meeting a few of these icons, thanking and congratulating them on their contributions and for helping to pave the way for the work that I am able to do today.

What should have been a great ending to an inspiring evening was instead marred by the attitudes and comments by some of the women who had been responsible for organizing and bringing these great women together in one room. Instead of congratulating each other and basking in their collective accomplishments, these women instead bickered about not being given equal time at the microphone or one person being given more acknowledgments than the other; and this was being played out in the presence of young female volunteers who came seeking to follow in their footsteps.

Collaboration is not about individual recognition, but rather it is about working together to achieve a collective goal. There will always be someone on top, in the middle and at the bottom of the process. The interesting thing about position is that in order to have a strong unit, it requires the support of them all. One position does not usurp the other and each is necessary to achieving a successful outcome.

When the goal is not achieved, everyone loses. And when everyone loses progress ceases.

Teaming to Win

1. **Find the right partner.** Collaborations work best when the right people come together as a team. Just as in marriage where compatibility is the key component to a successful union, such is the case too when choosing the right collaborator. In order to identify what is essential in the other person, it is just as, if not more important, to be able to recognize what key components you bring to the table.

   Teaming up with someone who compliments your strengths makes for an excellent team. For instance if you are introverted, identify that person who operates well out front and interacts effortlessly with other people.

   Identify someone who has the same value system as you as this will become important during those critical moments of decision-making. One sure-fire way to determine how this person might operate during those moments is to take the time to observe how they respond to other people in contentious situations. People are for the most part consistent in their behavior. Do not kid yourself into thinking that a person who is , for example, prone to easily losing her temper is going to react any differently toward you at a critical moment in your relationship. Pay attention to details regarding behavior and have the courage to walk away if it does not fit the bill.

   Some of my biggest regrets have come about as a result of me ignoring the important elements to the rules of engagement. What I observed about myself was my tendency to see what I desired in the person, rather than what actually existed. When you make the mistake of glossing over character flaws or glaring differences, you run the risk of derailing the success of the mission.

For this reason, personal friends are probably not the right choice for someone with whom you should collaborate in business. When we allow personal relationships to become a part of a business arrangement, lines can become easily blurred and emotional obligation interferes with critical decision making. There have been some successful instances of friends collaborating on business ventures, but generally speaking, it is not the best option if you are looking for a good outcome. Preserve your friendship by keeping your professional and personal life separate.

2. **Define roles.** Identifying what roles each person will play in the relationship is critical to keeping things on track and avoiding misunderstandings and interruptions as you work to build the partnership. This process should be a part of the initial planning before you begin to work together as a team. Gain understanding and agreement on how and who will make key decisions and make an effort to be respectful to the other person's authority. If you are entering into a business arrangement that involves running a business as partners, be sure to put everything in writing as to the roles and responsibilities of each person involved. This will lower the risk of conflict as you work to move forward as well as help to keep things on track.

Enter the discussion of defining individual roles with an open mind and with a willingness to compromise for the greater good.

3. **Develop a working plan.** By defining a clear road map for team members to follow at the outset of the relationship, you increase the chances of realizing success. There is an old saying that goes, "if you fail to plan, you plan to fail". This is accurate on many levels and is one of the many reasons why businesses or team collaborations fail.

   Talk through each aspect of the plan and allow each person to voice their individual concerns. In areas where you differ, compromise. Remain focused on what is important to the overall mission and steer clear of subjects that do not apply. Take the time to invest in the development of a good plan and watch your plans succeed. Remember, when you take the time to plan for the worst, chances are very good the worst will never happen. Keep in mind that in order to travel well and reach your destination, you must know where you are going.

4. **Identify a mediator.** Sometimes, no matter how well we plan, things can be thrown off track. One of the best ways to get things back on track quickly and with minimal damage is to have a plan in place to handle it before it happens. As a part of instituting safety nets, add to your list, a trusted and wise mediator. Ideally this person should not be friend, but rather a person who understands the overall mission and is willing and able to make the right decisions for the good of the mission should and when the need arises.

It should be agreed upon up front that whatever decision is made by the mediator that the decision will be final.

It is not uncommon for people to disagree on any given subject, but it is a wise woman who will plan her response to such a possibility, well in advance of the occurrence. When you anticipate and plan accordingly, you can almost be certain of a good outcome.

5. **Engage in honest and positive dialogue regularly.** Most misunderstandings come about as a result of things that are left unspoken or the failure to communicate effectively when they do. By making a commitment to discuss business concerns and issues in an open and honest forum, you reduce stress which is not uncommon when working with other people.

When things are left unsaid, people have a tendency to imagine the worst thereby turning what was perhaps a simple misunderstanding into something that has far-reaching repercussions. Take the opportunity to establish clear lines of communication and put good practices into place.

Establish ground rules for the discussions and agree to engage on a regular basis. When there is a difference of opinion, choose your word carefully before speaking and be vigilant in your efforts to not make things personal. Instead, maintain your focus and stay true to the mission.

Be careful not to communicate when angry or frustrated and make a concerted effort to listen to what other members of the team have to say. Remember, it is a team which means each team member has an equal say. Keep in mind also, that getting your way is not in the best interest of the team, so be willing to compromise.

Here are the key rules of verbal engagement:

Each person's opinion, whether in your estimation, it is right or wrong, deserves to be heard.

Never make it personal; either taking it personally or issuing a personal attack against the other person which will ultimately take your focus off of the point of the discussion. Keep it focused!

Listen and learn. When we listen we begin to gain a broader picture of how to live beyond ourselves and we also gain a clearer view of the world. By broadening our perspective, our ensuing actions are able to effect positive change in ourselves and in the people around us.

Gossip or malicious dialogue should never be a part of the discussion. As a gauge ask yourself these questions: *Is it fact, Is it constructive and Is it necessary to the end game?* If the answer is no, re-focus the discussion.

Begin the conversation with a stated purpose in order to keep the dialogue on point. Define what it is you hope to achieve at the conclusion of the discussion.

If the conversation warrants contentiousness, FIGHT FAIR. No hitting below the belt, in other words do not make it personal.

If you must criticize, use the sandwich approach. Begin and end each point with something positive.

Breathe! Very few things in life are ever as serious as we imagine them to be. And remember, you are in this collaboration to win, so keep your focus on the end game!

6. **Continue to evolve.** One of the best ways to grow a collaboration is to keep evolving the relationship in a positive direction. Make each new experience a building block upon which to establish new goals and expand toward greater opportunities.

   Establish a network of trusted advisors with diverse perspectives and experiences who can assist you with keeping your mission relative to the work that you are trying to accomplish. By doing this, you will reduce the risk of becoming complacent or irrelevant, consequently, improving your effectiveness. Be open to switching roles if the situation calls for a different approach but taking extra care not to infringe on the authority of the other parties.

7. **Be supportive of the other person's efforts.** One key benefit that comes with collaboration is having the availability of a ready-made support system. This support system is extremely critical to achieving the mission and can be the difference between reaching and failing to reach your goals.

   By supporting one another you are able to not only double your efforts, but you also double the impact.

Exercise

1. What are some of the key qualities found in a good collaboration?

   _____

   _____

   _____

   _____

   _____

2. What is a good way to go about defining roles in a collaborative relationship?

   _____

   _____

   _____

   _____

   _____

3. What are the key things needed to develop a good plan?

   _____

   _____

   _____

   _____

   _____

4. How do you find a good mediator and what attributes should you look for?

    _____

    _____

    _____

    _____

    _____

5. What are the key rules of verbal engagement?

    _____

    _____

    _____

    _____

    _____

6. Why is it important in a collaboration to keep evolving?

    _____

    _____

    _____

    _____

    _____

7. List ways in which you can be supportive to your collaboration partner(s).

_____

_____

_____

_____

_____

Chapter Seven

Unhealthy Competition

Competing to a Good End

"Winners compare their achievements
with their goals, while losers compare their
achievements with those of other people."
– Nido Qubein

It's Toxic

We can all run in the same direction, but if women are to reach our ultimate destination of empowerment, we cannot run over each other as a means of getting there. Competition is a part of life and is very healthy except when it is used to maliciously trample over other women. Women who compete by undermining or attacking the character of other women in order to advance themselves, do nothing to further their own cause, not to mention the cause of women in general.

It is a given that in order to excel, whether in business or on a personal level, competition is the ultimate motivation to help set things in motion.

Competition provides a bar by which to measure oneself. It separates mediocrity from excellence and helps to establish a platform for those who have the capacity to lead.

It is incumbent upon women to constantly assess their positions when competing and determine the most productive ways in which to engage.

Too often, women allow themselves to resort to tactics that destroy the very things that we fight so hard to build and as a result, we must revisit territory that has already been established.

When we allow ourselves to be sidetracked by personal feelings of insecurity, jealousy and bitterness towards other women, it sends the message that we are incapable of working together to get things done.

It is a fact and a great disappointment to know that men, who unfortunately are most of the decision makers when it comes to hiring or advancing women, are of the opinion that women, when teamed with other women are most likely to impede progress because of the challenges we have in working together effectively. This is a very sad commentary indeed, but once again, if we are to redefine what is perceived about us, we must first acknowledge and change what exists.

When women make the decision to completely focus on any given task or initiative, there is nothing more powerful on earth. We are masters of organization and details and our ability to see things through is unmatched. These are the qualities that make for great leaders. By putting ourselves in check and finally determining that there is nothing more important to the cause of women than to be in the position to lead, we acknowledge that this has to become our highest priority. This means we must walk, talk and lead like leaders.

Keeping it Fair

1. **Stay in your own lane.** Competition just for the sake of competing has a way of diminishing your own value. Resist the urge to hog the spotlight when it is another woman's moment to shine. Becoming someone who steps into spaces that have been hewn out by someone else simply because you have difficulty supporting another woman in her moment of celebration is not only unflattering to you, but it minimizes what she has managed to achieve and the achievements of women on a much broader scale.

   Take this opportunity to learn how to excel in your own space and by lending support, you will automatically build a supportive network for the things on your own personal horizon.

2. **Do not undermine another person's efforts.** There are two ways in which you can undermine a person. By actively inflicting harm upon their efforts or by sitting passively on the sidelines while others do and not lifting a hand to stop it. Either way the victim of such actions is harmed.

   Each woman has the responsibility to be the *keeper* or *helper* of other women. Our innate ability to nurture others is something that can be turned on or off at will. When we choose to turn on our care for other women, we boost the value of what we personally have to offer.

   Channel any negative feelings into supporting those women who can benefit from what you bring. What you will discover is in the process your value will increase as well.

3. **Avoid engaging in negative conversation with others.** One of the most common weapons used by women in competitive situations is the poison of negative conversation.

   Words have the power to destroy in ways that are far-reaching and long-lasting and can in a split second, polarize masses of people. This is especially a concern given the power of social media and how quickly negative messages can be distributed throughout multiple networks.

   By using the power of your own personal influence, you can change the conversation into one of empowering women as opposed to harming them. As a rule, if there is nothing good to share, change the topic of the conversation.

4. **Recognize and applaud the accomplishments of your competitor.** The primal nature of human beings is to destroy whatever they deem to be a threat to their existence or well-being. Although this is true of our nature on a basic level, we have the benefit of being an evolved species therefore we have the capacity to rise above and still this basic instinct, if we choose.

   Although the idea of competition suggests winning the prize, but it does not require that you destroy a competitor in the process.

When it is the moment for your competition to shine, take the opportunity to applaud her accomplishments. This is not only smart, but can also serve as a good strategy to elevate women in general. Each time a woman is elevated onto a more prominent platform, it allows other women to be placed in a position to take their achievements, at a minimum, into that space.

Resist the temptation to make negative commentary about what may or may not have contributed to her success. The only conversation that is of any importance is the acknowledgement that she did it.

5. **Steer clear of "cat fights".** Whether of a verbal or physical nature, "cat fights" are not a good look for empowered women. When you allow yourself to become embroiled in this kind of battle, you can be certain to emerge from the fight with lasting scars. No one wins in these kinds of situations. The sad news is in most of these encounters, the fight is not contained to just the people involved. Instead it demands that sides are chosen and it has the capacity to extend to audiences far beyond its original intended borders. The best course of action is to stifle it before it has a chance to catch fire.

6. **Learn from your competition.** One of the most fertile grounds on which to polish your skills is the ground occupied by the person in the leading position. The fact is, leaders learn from other leaders so don't miss your opportunity to learn how to lead.

To do this effectively, be transparent regarding your desire to one day follow in her footsteps. Be generous in your support and thank her for the opportunity to learn from such an accomplished leader.

7. **Do not make it personal.** Ask any woman on the planet the question of whether or not she has ever had a moment when she took the conversation off topic in favor of focusing on personal matters in critical moments and she will probably say yes. And to keep this discussion honest, I will be the first to say, I have.

Whether or not your competition has the body that you wish was yours is not important. What is important is the fact that you have been given the opportunity to engage another powerful woman with different ideas, approaches to life and, by the way, may be just the person you need in your corner to get you to where you are trying to land. When we allow ourselves to focus on such unimportant matters, we stunt the growth of women and limit the opportunity to expand what might be made available to us in the future.

You are different than every woman you will ever meet in life so get over it! It is our diversity that strengthens us rather than the other way around. If you choose to spend your life lamenting over things over which you have no control, be prepared to spend your life in helpless competition, in races that you will never win.

If your competition moves ahead of you in line, do not stoop to focusing on personal issues. Instead, choose to step into the fertile space that was once occupied by her before she advanced to higher ground.

Exercise

1. Define healthy competition?

_____

_____

_____

_____

_____

2. How can you avoid undermining women around you?

_____

_____

_____

_____

_____

3. How do you steer a negative conversation in a positive direction?

_____

_____

_____

_____

_____

4. What is the benefit to you in celebrating the accomplishments of someone who is a competitor?

_____

_____

_____

_____

_____

5. Why are "cat fights" so dangerous to trying to advance the cause of women?

_____

_____

_____

_____

_____

6. What positive things can you learn from your competition?

_____

_____

_____

_____

_____

7. What detriment is there in bringing personal feelings and opinions into a competitive environment?

_____

_____

_____

_____

_____

Afterword

Writing this book has been one of the toughest and most rewarding experiences ever. What made it so tough to write was the introspection that one must go through in order to write about a topic that, although is very broad in its spectrum, it is also very personal as it touches upon many aspects of my own personal journey to becoming the woman who exists inside of me today.

What became very telling concerning the importance of writing this book, were the responses of each person with whom I had the opportunity to talk to and ask questions regarding the subject of women and our relationships with and to each other. The responses were very impassioned and their opinions on this subject revealed much more than I could have ever imagined. I was encouraged by the number of women and their candid responses regarding many of their own experiences and why they think this work is so important to getting women to finally open up and talk about this painful, yet critical topic. These women seemed eager to be guided to the other side of this crisis and into a space that allows them to be the empowered women that we only dream about today.

Over the course of writing this book, I spent a fair amount of time reviewing research about various aspects of where women are today in regards to empowerment. And although this information proved to be very insightful, I chose not to clutter the pages with reference data that in the long run, does not answer the questions of WHY and HOW - do we finally become empowered. For the purposes of this work, the most important data is yet to be revealed by the women whose honest conversations I pray will now ensue.

This book is in no way a suggestion nor a claim to have all the answers, but rather, it is a bold attempt to pry open a door that has been sealed for far too long. It is my belief that by prying open this door, we will be able to begin the process of healing and working together as empowered women.

Healing requires not only pulling away the scabs of perhaps centuries of hurt and misunderstandings, but also applying the salve of forgiveness to both ourselves and the women who have been divinely placed in our lives to accompany us on our life journeys.

Dreams are wonderful, but at some point you have to wake up and deal with the reality of what is! We are here now, in this moment, so let the talking and healing begin!

Acknowledgements

Writing this book would never have been possible without the women and men who have encouraged me through the many ups and downs over a few decades of my life. Understanding such a complex topic does not come easily and much of the knowledge I have gained has come about as a result of having to endure and learn lessons which I care not to repeat.

I would like to thank my husband and children who without their love and support especially over the past few years, none of this would have been possible. You never stopped believing in the dream.

To my friend Eddy Cettina, thank you for being a model of what women do in support of each other. You have been a rock in my life and have loved and supported me even when I wanted to give up on myself.

And to Jackie Smith who over the years have been there for me and always willing and ready to support me in all of my endeavors. You epitomize what it means to be a h.e.l.p.e.r.!

To my friend Thomasina Shealey, whose home has been my refuge when I have needed to run away to still myself and for being the best traveling buddy ever. France awaits us!

To Donna, Harriet, Sandra, April Payne, and Mary Ross, you ladies know how to apply that salve of friendship and have been a healing balm for me over some pretty rough days.

To Wanda Boyd, Andrea Rock, my sisters Pamela and Sheila, and Maimah, thank you for listening and praying for me.

To the loveliest couple I know, Bob and Irma Bogan, thank you for your love and support.

To Mikki Taylor, for the hills and valleys that have granted us both access to wisdom, thank you.

To Jacqueline Richardson, for being a strong pillar to lean on when I needed it most, thank you!

To the women who inspire and support me daily, Lydia Baugh and Enid Doggett, thank you!

To Jessica Grounds, whose conversation inspired me to finish what I started, I will be forever in your debt.

Thanks also to Barbara Jacksier whom since first meeting you, have jumped in with both feet in support of my efforts.

There are so many others who have been an encouragement throughout this process of getting me here and so to those whose names are not mentioned, THANK YOU!

And to the God of all who loves me enough to let me be me, I give my highest praise!

Resource Guide

Levo League –www.levoleague.com

Levo League is a thriving online and offline community of young professionals, mentors, and innovative companies taking Gen Y by storm. Levo League's mission is to help professional women elevate their careers by providing the best job opportunities, skill building tools and networking connections to accelerate their success. Elevate your career at levoleague.com.

Running Start – www.runningstartonline.com

Founded in early 2007, Running Start grew out of the non-partisan Women Under Forty Political Action Committee (WUFPAC), which financially supports young women running for federal office. Running Start was formed when it became clear that the pool of young women considering careers in politics and running for elected office was far too small. Young women and girls need to be educated about politics earlier in life if the make-up of the political leaders in our country is to transform. We must instill in the next generation that public service is admirable and achievable. Running Start provides young women and girls with the skills and confidence they need to become the political leaders of tomorrow.

Running Start supports the young women who will shape tomorrow's world. We aim to plant the seed of interest in politics so that they will run earlier, climb higher through leadership, and share more in the decision making power of their country. These young women will bring in new ideas to help solve old problems, and will raise issues unique to their lives that have otherwise been overlooked in politics.

We founded Running Start to address the absence of equal representation in the halls of government. We continue to educate and inspire around the pillars of our mission.

Tigerlily Foundation www.tigerlilyfoundation.org

Tigerlily Foundation was founded by Maimah Karmo, after she was diagnosed with breast cancer at 32 years old.

Maimah is committed to educating young women around the world about breast cancer; and empowering them to be their own best advocates. She is dedicated to changing the young adult breast cancer landscape and seeks to impact the quality of care and lifestyle for young women affected by this disease.

She chose to name the organization Tigerlily because like a flower loses its petals in the Fall and Winter, then blossoms and grows in the Spring and Summer, a woman undergoing treatment can also find her true beauty, strength and be transformed during and after breast cancer.

The Stargazer Lily, her personal favorite, is prized for its elegance. It is known for its heady fragrance and bold, beautiful colors. Like a woman, lilies are never dormant. They bloom and survive in all seasons. That is her and our wish for the young women we serve – that despite breast cancer, they can thrive.

Ladies America www.ladiesamerica.org

Ladies America began in Washington, D.C. as Ladies Dinner Club, a simple dinner meeting opportunity for professional women to gather outside of work and form viable relationships. Ladies America Founder, Lindsey Mask, made a personal effort to connect with professional women in a purposeful way and to combat the theory women could not work together and alleviate the slippery slope mentality. Her goal of having a non-competitive forum for women to connect drew thousands of women to join, where they abide by the motto, "Women Helping Women." With backing from extensive networks of women across the country, Ladies DC organically evolved into a fully functioning national network with subsequent boards, partnerships, sponsorships, mentorship programs, education platforms and business partnerships. With the creation of chapters across the country, Ladies America was born, which now has seven chapters across the country. The group now incorporates two initiatives a year: 2012: Women in Technology & Women in Global Economics; 2013: Women in Military & Salary Negotiation; and hosts an annual women's conference, "Women Leading the Future."

MEMBERS

While we do not have limitations of age or profession for members, we have found that typical demographic includes women ages 23-45 with undergraduate, graduate, or Ph.D degrees. Ladies America members are successful women in a variety of industries, including business, politics, education, design, art, finance, associations, marketing and communications, law, and there are several business owners.

Girls Incorporated www.girlsinc.org

Girls Inc. inspires all girls to be strong, smart, and bold through life-changing programs and experiences that help girls navigate gender, economic, and social barriers. Research-based curricula, delivered by trained, mentoring professionals in a positive all-girl environment equip girls to achieve academically; lead healthy and physically active lives; manage money; navigate media messages; and discover an interest in science, technology, engineering, and math. The network of local Girls Inc. nonprofit organizations serves 136,000 girls ages 6 - 18 annually across the United States and Canada.

Our History The Girls Inc movement started in New England during the Industrial Revolution as a response to the needs of a new working class: young women who had migrated from rural communities in search of newly available job opportunities in textile mills and factories.

Programs Girls Inc develops research-based informal education programs that encourage girls to take risks and master physical, intellectual and emotional challenges. Major programs address math and science education, pregnancy and drug abuse prevention, media literacy, economic literacy, adolescent health, violence prevention, and sports participation.

National Board and CEO Our national leadership focuses on developing innovative ways to leverage our most valuable asset—acknowledged expertise as the nation's premiere program provider and advocate for girls—to expand our reach. Our leaders include Ellen Stafford-Sigg, National

Board Chair; and Donna Brace Ogilvie, National Board Honorary Chair.

Funding Girls Inc. is committed to maximizing our resources in benefit of the girls we serve and efficient use of our funding. 84% of our expenses go directly to programming.

Membership Girls Inc. programming can be offered anywhere girls are found, including Girls Inc. centers, schools, churches, community centers and housing projects. The majority of Girls Inc. centers are located in low–income areas and provide a weekly average of 30 hours of after-school, weekend and summer activities.

Research The National Resource Center (NRC) is the organization's research, information services and training site. Research and evaluation conducted by the NRC provide the foundation for Girls Inc. programs. The NRC also responds to requests for information on girls' issues and distributes Girls Inc. publications.

Advocacy Girls Inc informs policymakers about girls' needs locally and nationally. The organization educates the media about critical issues facing girls. In addition, the organization teaches girls how to advocate for themselves and their communities, using their voices to promote positive change.

National Scholars The Girls Inc Scholars Program was created in 1992 when Lucile Miller Wright, a longtime supporter of Girls Incorporated, bequeathed $6.4 million from her estate to the organization to fund scholarships expressly for young women members. This endowed fund secures the base of a commitment to scholarships at Girls Incorporated that began in 1945 with the Reader's Digest Career Key program.

Ms. Foundation for Women – www.forwomen.org

Forty years ago, four visionary women established the Ms. Foundation for Women to elevate women's voices and create positive change. Today, we're a dynamic and powerful entity that is leading the charge on women's issues nationwide.

This is how we do it.

We start with the knowledge that our fight is not yet over. It's true that women have come a long way since the 1970s, but for every woman who has reached the "top" (and who still face discrimination, by the way), there are millions of women struggling to earn a living wage, gain access to basic health care, secure affordable child care and participate in the opportunities that should be available to every person in the U.S.

At the Ms. Foundation, we work to bring attention to the real challenges facing women, especially women of color and low-income women, living in poverty, working paycheck to paycheck or both. We tirelessly advocate for national and statewide policy change that will address these challenges, and we support more than 100 organizations throughout the country that are working for change on a grassroots level.

We are committed. We are motivated. And we will not stop. Not until all women enjoy true equality, equity and opportunity.

Vital Voices Global Partnership – www. forwomen.org

Our mission is to identify, invest in and bring visibility to extraordinary women around the world by unleashing their leadership potential to transform lives and accelerate peace and prosperity in their communities.

Vital Voices Global Partnership is the preeminent non-governmental organization (NGO) that identifies, trains and empowers emerging women leaders and social entrepreneurs around the globe, enabling them to create a better world for us all.

We are at the forefront of international coalitions to combat human trafficking and other forms of violence against women and girls.

We enable women to become change agents in their governments, advocates for social justice, and supporters of democracy and the rule of law.

We equip women with management, business development, marketing, and communications skills to expand their enterprises, help to provide for their families, and create jobs in their communities.

Our international staff and team of over 1,000 partners, pro bono experts and leaders, including senior government, corporate and NGO executives, have trained and mentored more than 14,000 emerging women leaders from over 144 countries in Africa, Asia, Eurasia, Latin America and the

Caribbean, and the Middle East since 1997. These women have returned home to train and mentor more than 500,000 additional women and girls in their communities. They are the Vital Voices of our time.

Black Girls Rock – info@blackgirlsrockinc.com

BLACK GIRLS ROCK! Inc. is 501(c)3 non-profit youth empowerment and mentoring organization established to promote the arts for young women of color, as well as to encourage dialogue and analysis of the ways women of color are portrayed in the media.

Since 2006, BLACK GIRLS ROCK! has been dedicated to the healthy development of young women and girls. BLACK GIRLS ROCK! seeks to build the self-esteem and self-worth of young women of color by changing their outlook on life, broadening their horizons, and helping them to empower themselves. Since 2006, we have enjoyed the opportunity to enrich the lives of girls aged 12 to 17 years old through mentorship, arts education, cultural exploration and public service. At BLACK GIRLS ROCK!, young women are offered access to enrichment programs and opportunities that place special emphasis on personal development through the arts and cooperative learning.

By speaking to the next generation in their formative years about issues of self-worth, goals, and aspirations, the organization reinforces the message that young women need not objectify themselves or relinquish their autonomy. BLACK GIRLS ROCK! has boldly taken on the crisis of our female youth of color here in America head on and understands the need for positive self-images and a strong sense of awareness. WE SEE SOLUTIONS.

Womensphere www.womensphere.org

Womensphere is a unique leadership community and global social enterprise that brings together people, networks, companies, and institutions around the shared purpose of unleashing women's potential. We build ventures and collaborations dedicated to advancing women's evolution as leaders, innovators, entrepreneurs, and creators in our global society.

These are the principles and philosophy underlying the work that we do:

We believe that we create the reality that we experience - and therefore, we have the power to create a better future for women and for the world. We take a very proactive position in mobilizing people, resources, and technology to shape outcomes towards advancing women's evolution as leaders, innovators, entrepreneurs, and creators, and towards enabling women to achieving and fulfilling potential.

We believe that positive global transformation starts with the self. We must become the change that we seek. We believe that the seeds of change and solutions to the problems that beset humanity rest within us.

We believe that unlocking women's full potential is necessary to advancing the evolution of our global society. We believe in the critical, catalytic role that women play in transforming the world. At Womensphere, we actively invest in unlocking women's full potential and enabling women to succeed – as leaders of personal lives, of careers and organizations, of communities, and of the world.

We believe in the power of diversity to fuel innovation and creative solutions. The sphere would not exist without the circles that comprise it, and a circle on its own cannot create a sphere. We believe that in order to truly unleash potential in oneself and others, to inspire positive transformation, to solve problems, and to create positive impact in the world – the great ideas and great leaders of our time will come from a diversity of disciplines, industries, nationalities, cultures, affiliations, generations, and backgrounds. We believe that the power of unity and collaboration of many different circles, will result in ultimately greater outcomes for women and for humanity.

We believe in the power of community to build and nurture positive change. Innovation has made this an era when individual power is at its greatest – any one person can have a voice, inspire change, and affect outcomes. We believe that success and positive change endures when a community is behind it. Thus, we believe in building, nurturing, and inspiring collaboration among a community of leaders – bringing together women and men, emerging leaders, academic institutions, networks, companies, governments, and many institutions that share our mission and purpose.

We believe that it is our individual and collective responsibility and purpose to create better realities for ourselves, for the people we care about, and for humanity – in the present and in the future.

Our work at Womensphere is an expression of these principles and philosophy.

One Billion Rising – www.onebillionrising.org

ONE BILLION RISING FOR JUSTICE is a global call to women survivors of violence and those who love them to gather safely in community outside places where they are entitled to justice – court houses, police stations, government offices, school administration buildings, work places, sites of environmental injustice, military courts, embassies, places of worship, homes, or simply public gathering places where women deserve to feel safe but too often do not. It is a call to survivors to break the silence and release their stories – politically, spiritually, outrageously – through art, dance, marches, ritual, song, spoken word, testimonies and whatever way feels right.

Our stories have been buried, denied, erased, altered, and minimized by patriarchal systems that allow impunity to reign. Justice begins when we speak, release, and acknowledge the truth in solidarity and community. ONE BILLION RISING FOR JUSTICE is an invitation to break free from confinement, obligation, shame, guilt, grief, pain, humiliation, rage, and bondage.

The campaign is a recognition that we cannot end violence against women without looking at the intersection of poverty, racism, war, the plunder of the environment, capitalism, imperialism, and patriarchy. Impunity lives at the heart of these interlocking forces.

American Association of University Women www.aauw.org

The American Association of University Women (AAUW) is the nation's leading voice promoting equity and education for women and girls. Since our founding in 1881, AAUW members have examined and taken positions on the fundamental issues of the day — educational, social, economic, and political.

Since its first meeting in 1881, AAUW has been a catalyst for change. Our nonpartisan, nonprofit organization has more than 165,000 members and supporters across the United States, as well as 1,000 local branches and 800 college and university partners. Throughout our history, AAUW members have examined and taken positions on the fundamental issues of the day — educational, social, economic, and political. This online collection of AAUW milestones tells the story of AAUW's important role in women's history.

What started with 17 like-minded women has grown into a powerful network that has influenced — and at times shaped — the debate over equity in education.

Success In The City

What you need to know:

Success in the City (SITC) is an executive women's organization for smart, unique, and driven women. We are a community focused on celebrating women's success and accomplishments and providing a rich network of shared experiences, and professional resources. A SITC woman has a strong entrepreneurial spirit and seeks to cultivate community, share wisdom, and foster knowledge with other accomplished women.

Our Vision:

We are by, for and about women business leaders who desire and deserve a unique community experience.

Where we are today:

Today, Success in the City is comprised of some of the most influential women business leaders in the Metro D.C. Area. With a dedicated membership, we have established a place where friendships come first, business booms, and laughter is always in style.

How all this started:

It started as a one-time, over-the-top event; a farewell to the show that defined sass and style, HBO's "Sex and the City." But, there was one rule required in order to attend – wear red lipstick and stilettos. As 70 of Washington's women wandered upstairs to the luxurious Tower Club, something special started to happen. Laughs became more boisterous, stories became more intimate, and sincere friendships started to form. By the time the evening ended, every attendee pleaded with the organizer, Cynthia de Lorenzi, for more.

So, Cynthia took her Texan "bigger is better" attitude and began organizing razzle-dazzle events all over the D.C. area. Within a year, it was clear – women not only wanted, but needed a place where they could express their fabulousness. Those initial friendships that formed started turning into big business deals. And again, attendees started begging for more.

The uniqueness of Success in the City has not gone unnoticed since it launched as a bona fide member organization in 2008. The Washington Post called Success in the City The Pink Collar Network. Since the launch of Success in the City in 2008, the organization has grown to more than 4,000 avid followers and is looking forward to launching chapters in cities across the U.S. and even internationally in the coming years.

Today, Success in the City is comprised of some of the most influential business leaders in the Metro D.C. Area. We have laid claim as a place where friendships come first, business booms, and fun is always in style.

Women Are Talking – www.womenaretalking.org

Our Vision:

Women Are Talking envisions a world where women talk with one another to share resources, learn, and benefit from the experiences of other women so that women can create what's important to them and do it on their own terms.

Our Mission:

The mission of Women Are Talking is to create an easily-accessible space where women can support one another through sharing knowledge, experiences, and resources.

Our Concept:

Women Are Talking is a virtual interactive space where women of all walks of life can connect via the WAT interactive website to support one another in their respective efforts.

Each year in May women from around the globe convene using the power of technology to talk about issues that concern women. They do this by utilizing an interactive website, social media and the internet. These discussions result in a call to action that will engage the proper resources in order to find solutions for identified issues. These discussions/conversations will be moderated in different cities around the country and abroad by women leaders who bring knowledge and experience on the topics identified within our framework.

The interactive site will serve as an aggregator in order to connect women with women from various organizations, businesses and individuals who are seeking answers in order to share resources and direction.